Albert Einstein

Michael Alcott

Published in association with The Basic Skills Agency

Hodder & Stoughton

A MEMBER OF THE HODDER HEADLINE

Acknowledgements

Cover: Topham Picturepoint

Illustrations: Mike Bell

Photos: Topham Picturepoint

Every effort has been made to trace copyright holders of material reproduced in this book. Any rights not acknowledged will be acknowledged in subsequent printings if notice is given to the publisher.

Orders; please contact Bookpoint Ltd, 39 Milton Park, Abingdon, Oxon OX14 4TD. Telephone: (44) 01235 400414, Fax: (44) 01235 400454. Lines are open from 9.00–6.00, Monday to Saturday, with a 24 hour message answering service. Email address: orders@bookpoint.co.uk

British Library Cataloguing in Publication Data
A catalogue record for this title is available from the British Library

ISBN 0 340 77617 X

First published 2000
Impression number   10 9 8 7 6 5 4 3 2 1
Year   2005 2004 2003 2002 2001 2000

Typeset by GreenGate Publishing Services, Tonbridge, Kent.
Printed in Great Britain for Hodder and Stoughton Educational, a division of Hodder Headline Plc, 338 Euston Road, London NW1 3BH, by Redwood Books, Trowbridge, Wilts

Contents

Albert Einstein

1 Childhood

Albert Einstein was born in 1879 in Ulm, Germany.
'His head is a funny shape,' said his mother.
'Don't worry,' said the doctor.
'It will be all right.'

His mother and father were Jewish.
This was to be a very important fact in Albert's life.

When their son was a year old the family moved.
They went to live in Munich,
another town in Germany.
This was the first of many moves
that Albert was to make in his life.
In Munich, his father set up an engineering factory.

Albert Einstein with his sister

Albert was a quiet little boy.
He did not speak until he was three.
'There must be something wrong with him,'
people said.
But there was nothing wrong.
He liked to say things over and over in his head
to get them right.
Then he would speak out loud.

He was pleased when his sister was born.

Her name was Maria.
'Where are the wheels?' he asked.
He thought that a sister would be a new toy.

He never played with toy soldiers.
'I hate soldiers. I hate war,' he said.
He was to hate war all his life.

Albert's mother loved music.
'You must learn the violin,' she told him.
He did not enjoy violin lessons
but he had to learn to play.
As an adult, he loved the violin
and played it in concerts.

When he was four years old,
Albert went to a Catholic school.
He was the only Jewish boy there.
The teachers were very strict
and Albert was unhappy.

One day, when he was five, Albert fell ill.
He had to stay in bed.
'Here is a present for you,' said his father
when he came home from work.
Albert held the flat, round object in his hands.
'What is it?' he asked.
'A compass.'
'What does it do?'
His father took the compass
and placed it on his own hand.
'See. The needle points to the north.'
'How does it do that?'
'It is magnetic,' said his father.

This was the start of Albert's interest in science.
All his life, he would ask how things worked.

At secondary school
Albert's favourite subject was maths.
An uncle used to set geometry puzzles for him.
He enjoyed doing the puzzles.

Albert loved doing geometry puzzles.

When Albert was fifteen years old
he had a nasty shock.
One evening his father asked to see him.
Albert saw that his father was very worried.
'I have a serious problem,' said his father.
'My factory is not doing well. I must close it.
I am going to Italy with your mother and sister.'

'What about me ?' asked Albert.

'You must stay at school here in Germany.'

Albert saw his family leave for Italy.
He was very sad.
He had to live in a small hotel on his own.

At school he got into trouble.
One day the Head of the school asked to see him.
'Einstein, you are a trouble maker.
You must leave the school.'

Alone, and expelled from school,
Albert Einstein had a big problem.

2 Teenage Rebel

'Albert! What are you doing here ?'
The unhappy teenager stood at the door
of the house in Milan, Italy.
He saw that his mother was very surprised
to see him there. 'I have left school.'

His father was angry with him.
'What are you going to do?'

'Travel round Italy,' replied Albert.
He visited many cities and enjoyed the art of Italy.

He had another big surprise for his parents.
Over dinner one evening he told them.

'I do not want to be a German.'
'Pardon?' said his father, not believing his ears.
'I hate war. I am a pacifist. I believe in peace.
I do not want to do military service in Germany.'
'What will you become?' asked his mother.
'Nothing.'

His parents looked at each other in astonishment.
Five years later
Albert became a citizen of Switzerland,
so he never had to do military service after all.

Another time, his father talked to him
about his career plans.
'You can train to be an engineer,' said his father.
'I don't want to be an engineer.'
'What do you want to be?'
'I don't know. A teacher maybe.
I like maths and physics.'

So he went to Zurich Technology Institute
in Switzerland.

Albert studied physics.

13

He fell in love with Mileva, a student from Hungary.

One morning, Albert saw that she was very serious.
'What is it?' he asked.
'1 am pregnant.' said Mileva.

In February 1899, Mileva gave birth to a daughter.
She was a lovely baby.
But they could not keep her.
The baby was adopted and they never saw her again.

3 Becoming a Scientist

Albert was now twenty-two years old.
He had passed his exams. He needed a job.
It was difficult for Jewish people to get jobs.
Finally after two years he got a job.

The job was in the Patent Office in Berne,
a town in Switzerland.
'What will I do?' he asked at the interview.
'People invent things.' the manager said.
'You will check them to see if they are really new.'

It wasn't what Albert wanted to do
but he was desperate for a job.
But he began to enjoy the job.
He stayed there for seven years.

Life began to go well.
In 1903 he and Mileva married.
Their son, Hans, was born the next year.
A second son, Eduard, was born in 1910.

In his spare time Albert studied physics.
He began to make important discoveries.
He wrote about light and time and gravity.
Some scientists laughed at his strange ideas.
But he did not give up.

In 1905 he wrote a very important scientific paper,
The Special Theory of Relativity.
This made him famous even though
only a few people could understand his ideas.

He soon became a professor at
Berlin University
in Germany.
He was very pleased.

When he was a boy his mother had said
'One day, Albert, you will become a
university professor.'
It had come true.

His career as a scientist was now doing well.
But his marriage was not so good.
He separated from his wife, Mileva.
She went to live in Switzerland with their two sons.

When the First World War broke out in 1914,
he was living alone in a small flat in Berlin.
He hated the war.
He joined the Peace Movement.
Jewish people were attacked.
There was even an Anti-Einstein group.
This upset him a lot.

Albert making a television documentary at his home in
New Jersey.

In 1919 he divorced Mileva
and married his cousin, Elsa.
He continued to make discoveries in physics.
He also spent time helping Jewish people.
He played his violin at concerts
to raise money for poor Jews.
He supported the idea of a country for
Jewish people.

In 1921 he won the Nobel Prize for physics.
He was now world famous as a scientist.
People said he was a genius.

In 1921 Albert won the Nobel Prize for physics.

In the same year a man tried to murder him
because he was Jewish.
Now the Nazis were becoming more
and more powerful in Germany.
They were cruel to all Jewish people.

Life in Germany became very dangerous
for Albert Einstein even though he was
the most famous scientist in the world.
He and Elsa were frightened.
They had to escape.

In 1932 they made their decision.
They would leave Germany.
'Take a good look at our house,' he said to his wife.
'Why?' asked Elsa.
'We shall never see it again.'
He was right.
They would never return to Germany.

The Nazis attacked Jewish people and burned books written by Jews.

4 Living in Exile

Albert Einstein and his wife, Elsa,
went to live in the USA.
He worked as a professor at Princeton University.
Three years later Elsa died.
Then his sister, Maria, came to live with him.

The news from Germany was bad.
Hitler had become Leader of the country.
The Nazis attacked Jewish people.
They called Einstein a national enemy.
They smashed up his house in Berlin
and burned his books in public.

In 1941, Einstein became an American citizen.

As the Second World War came closer,
he was a very worried man.
He had made an important discovery about energy.
The world famous formula, $E = mc^2$
could help the Nazis to make a nuclear bomb.
He warned the American President.

But there was a terrible shock in store for him.
In 1945 two atomic bombs were dropped on Japan
by the Americans.

For the rest of his life
Einstein worked for world peace.
He asked rich countries to help poor countries.
He worked to create a country for Jewish people.

In 1948 one of his dreams came true.
Now the Jewish people had their own country.
Israel was created.
Einstein was asked to be President.
'No thank you,' he replied. 'I am too old now.'

A few years later, he was taken ill.
In hospital he refused any special treatment.
'It is time to go,' he said to the doctors and nurses.
He died on 18 April 1955.
He was seventy-six years old.

For the rest of his life, Albert Einstein worked for world peace.
Here he is at the Albert Hall, London, in 1933.